GAUGUIN

THE GREAT ARTISTS COLLECTION

MASON CREST

Contents

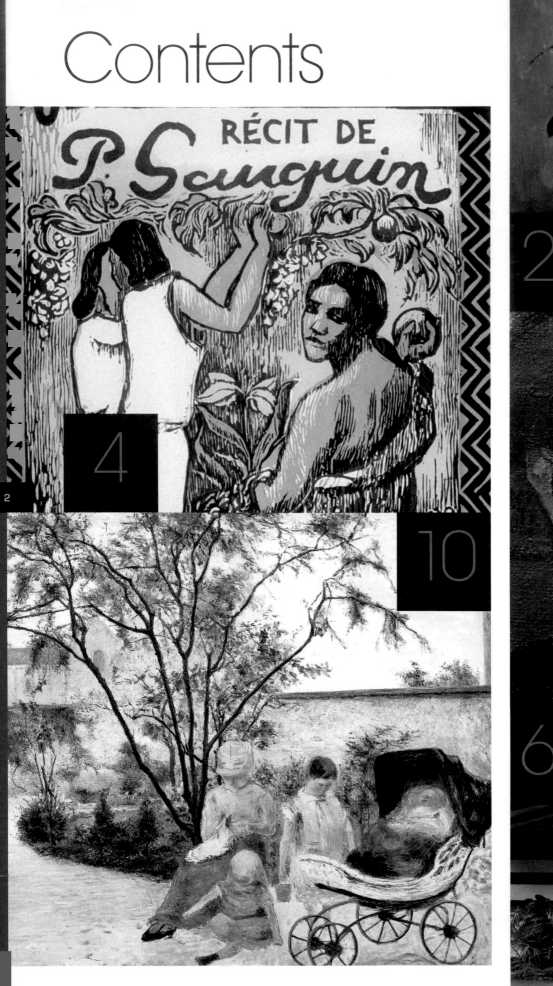

*Great Works order is alphabetical where possible.

GAUGUIN

Mason Crest
450 Parkway Drive, Suite D
Broomall, PA 19008
www.masoncrest.com

Printed and bound in the United States of America.

10 9 8 7 6 5 4 3 2 1

Cataloging-in-Publication Data on file with the Library of Congress.

Series ISBN: 978-1-4222-3256-9
Hardback ISBN: 978-1-4222-3259-0
ebook ISBN: 978-1-4222-8536-7

Written by: Sara Haynes

Images courtesy of PA Photos and Scala Archives

"The history of modern art is also the history of the progressive loss of art's audience. Art has increasingly become the concern of the artist and the bafflement of the public."

Paul Gauguin

Introduction

(Anders Beer Wilse/Norwegian Museum of Cultural History)

■ **ABOVE:** Paul Gauguin, c. 1891.

Paul Gauguin, along with other Post-Impressionist painters, was instrumental in a fundamental move toward a modernism not seen in art since the Impressionists themselves took shape. He believed in Paul Cézanne's geometric simplicity with its cones, spheres, and cylinders, but he also believed in himself, his own abilities, and the potential he had to become a great artist. Gauguin was confident he was a great artist – a form of genius – and he was unafraid to push the boundaries of art history with a move away from the traditional into a world of daring, insight, and paintings that could be regarded as well before their time.

Gauguin was also an industrious engraver and regularly worked with woodcuts; he became particularly influential in these mediums well into the 20th century. Woodcuts were first developed in the 5th century in China as a way of applying designs to textiles. The medium consists of hollowing an engraving in a piece of wood to form a design or illustration. Ink is then applied and the wood pressed on to paper in order to transfer the design. Wood engraving took over from woodcuts in the early 1800s, but there was a revival of the art toward the end of the 19th century – employed by the likes of Gauguin, who used the technique for the illustrations in his book, *Noa Noa*. However, in reality, woodcutting and engraving had already been outdated by lithography and photography for mass production.

Gauguin developed his paintings through many different stages and found inspiration across the globe, particularly in Paris, Brittany, and Arles in France, and the South Pacific. He began his painting career in Europe during the later part of the 19th century at a time when huge industrial technological change was taking place. While some artists reveled in these new developments, which included airplanes, the telephone, and the introduction of automobiles, Gauguin was less impressed with these technological advances and veered away from what he saw as a "modern" world – however, he was embarking on new innovations of his own. As the landscape in and around Paris began to change, the Impressionists were finding quality in the new cityscapes that were springing up, and although Gauguin used an Impressionist style for a time with patches of color applied through large brushstrokes, he resisted the changing modernized world and chose instead a simpler, less-cluttered approach by focusing on the pre-industrial age.

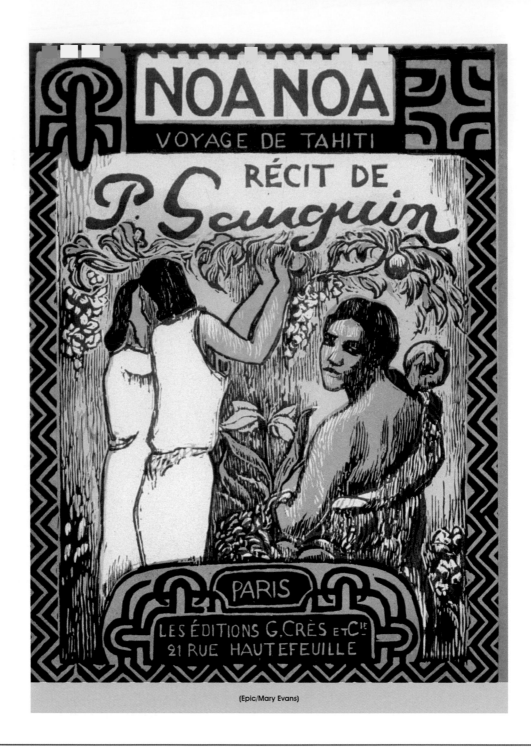

■ **ABOVE:** The cover of Gauguin's book *Noa Noa*, 1924.

As cities like Paris grew and developed, Gauguin chose to base himself in the French countryside where a more rural way of life suited his palette and the life he wished to capture through his oils. Later, this search for a more primitive existence would lead him to the South Pacific and Tahiti before he finally found himself in the Marquesas Islands in French Polynesia.

His period of association, collaboration, and friendship with Vincent Van Gogh is probably one of the most important times in Gauguin's life. It may have been just nine weeks at the Studio of the South – Van Gogh's vision for a group of likeminded artists – and there may have been only two of them, but the time these artists spent together, before they violently quarreled, was to prove invaluable in the history and development of art.

Hoping to encourage Claude Monet (1840-1926), Émile Bernard (1868-1941), and Camille Pissarro (1830-1903) to help him create an art school alongside Gauguin, Van Gogh moved to Arles in the south of France where he was convinced that modern art required bold, outlandish, color combinations. Gauguin did join Van Gogh in Arles and the two artists worked side by side, and Vincent painted sunflowers to decorate his friend's bedroom. It was these bold paintings that would help to make Van Gogh the influential artist for which he would become recognized. However, the artist's mental illness began to take a determined hold in 1888, and after threatening Gauguin with a knife, the two men parted company (following a spell of hospitalization for Van Gogh) although they remained in touch by letter sporadically for the remainder of Van Gogh's life. On the same day that Van Gogh attacked Gauguin he also mutilated his own earlobe and offered it to a prostitute as a gift.

It was not uncommon for Gauguin to include works of art behind his alluring self-portraits – perhaps as a means of introducing his subjects from his travels to an audience who little understood him. Today, his works are known as Symbolist art – an idealization and romanticism designed to express emotions, desires, and experiences. It was developed to show more about the artist and their work, than it had to do with painting within a realistic concept. This was particularly revolutionary for the time, and perhaps goes some way to understanding why Gauguin was not as highly revered and celebrated as he is today.

This partly came about because Gauguin found it constricting to paint from nature and to work outside (*en plein air*) – he liked to stretch the reality of any given piece. The resulting development was that Gauguin helped establish a new form of modern art through Post-Impressionism by using blocks of flat bright colors conveyed within dark outlines. These heavy outlines were to separate his works from those of his contemporaries. Impressionism was concerned with blending colors and pieces together in order to achieve a sense of time within the painting. Gauguin did the opposite and separated out his subjects with bold outlines instead. These were usually achieved by watering down Prussian blue paint, where the idea was to use the outline to emphasize the intensity of the colors within. Van Gogh was convinced that a "colorist" would provide the transition to modern art (he had no idea that he would actually be that colorist). Having moved away from the darker palettes of his earlier works, such as *The Potato Eaters*, he wrote at length to his brother Theo Van Gogh – also his closest friend, confidant, and supporter – about the advent of color. Gauguin was equally concerned with color, and, as well as Prussian blue, was particularly taken with cobalt blue, chrome yellow, red ochre, cobalt violet, cadmium yellow, zinc white, and emerald green.

The term Synthetism is widely associated with Gauguin

(Mary Evans Picture Library)

■ **ABOVE:** A portrait of Vincent Van Gogh who was a close friend of Paul Gauguin.

and other experimental artists. Also known as Cloisonnism, the movement began in Pont-Aven. A cloisonné was an early form of metalwork – popular in China and Japan – that involved using metal strips or wires to separate colors on vases and other ornaments. Gauguin transferred the idea to paintings, using bold outlines, and the term Cloisonnism was coined by the art critic Édouard Dujardin in 1888 to describe this modernist art movement. The style lasted from this time until the death of Gauguin in the early 1900s, whose best work to include the medium is *Vision after the Sermon: Jacob Wrestling with the Angel*, 1888. Gauguin was not alone in its use and other well-known artists to use Cloisonnism include Bernard, his good friend, Jacob Meyer de Haan, Louis Anquetin, and Paul Ranson. Gauguin did not have a term for his overall style, however, and Post-Impressionism was not coined until Roger Fry, celebrating the likes of Gauguin and Cézanne at a high-profile art exhibition at the Grafton Gallery in London, which opened in November 1910, used the term to describe the young French artists whom he was hoping to promote, alongside Manet, to a fresh, new audience. Whatever term Gauguin might have used for his own works, he helped to push the boundaries of Impressionism in a new direction which, now known as Post-Impressionism, was to last from the mid-1880s to the early 1900s. The new movement included a number of painters who exaggerated their Impressionistic roots and "invented" other mediums, including Expressionism, Pointillism, Pictorialism, Cloisonnism, the Nabis, Intimist, and Fauvism. It was revolutionary, it was experimental, and it was exciting. It broke away from tradition, pushed the boundaries of acceptability, and moved art history in a direction from which modern art would develop toward contemporary art in the mid-20th century. Gauguin played an essential part in this development by creating something new and fresh, extending the parameters of art and showing foresight to an art industry and public that were, sadly, not quite ready for him.

(Mary Evans/Epic/Tallandier)

■ **ABOVE: A portrait of painter Émile Bernard (1868-1941) by Toulouse-Lautrec. Bernard was a close friend of Gauguin.**

■ **OPPOSITE: Gazers at paintings few appreciate and fewer understand: Sketches of the 1910-1911 Manet and the Post-Impressionists Exhibition at the Grafton Gallery in London. This controversial exhibition introduced modern art to Britain and was organized and curated by Roger Fry.**

POST-IMPRESSIONIST EXPRESSIONS—SKETCHES BY FRANK REYNOLDS.

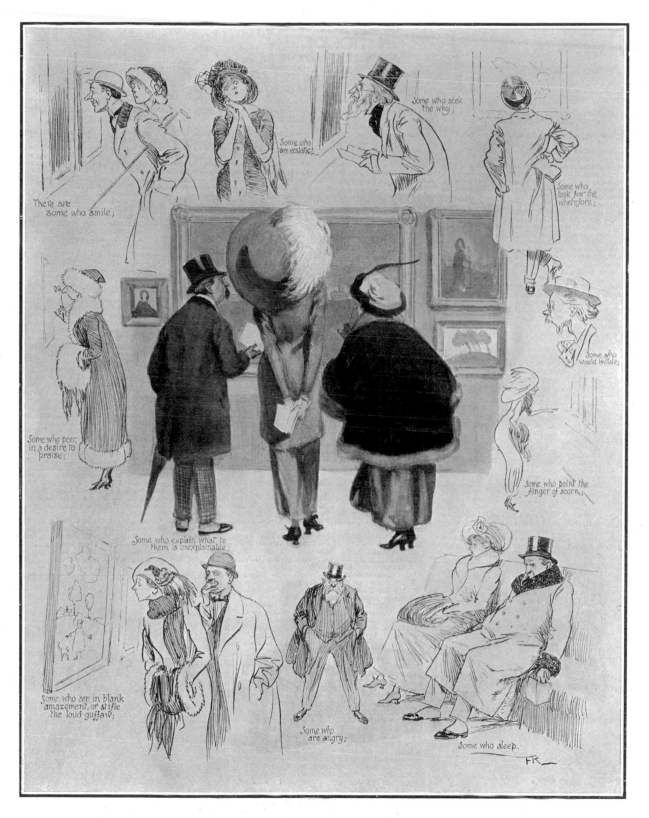

GAZERS AT PAINTINGS FEW APPRECIATE AND FEWER UNDERSTAND: STUDIES AT THE GRAFTON GALLERIES.

The Exhibition of pictures by Manet and the Post-Impressionists, as we noted in our issue of last week under a number of reproductions of examples, is attracting all London to the Grafton Galleries. Without unfairness, it may be said that the success of the show is in large measure a success of curiosity. To the few who appreciate and understand the work there are many who do neither, who go merely to gaze and scoff, and to feel that they have been in the new movement, if not of it.

Gauguin
A Biography

■ **ABOVE:** The family of Paul Gauguin in the garden of their home in Copenhagen c. 1873-1883.

Eugène Henri Paul Gauguin, known as Paul, was born in Paris, France, to Clovis Gauguin, a journalist, and Aline Maria Chazal on June 7, 1848. It was also the year that the 1848 Revolution (Third French Revolution) began, part of a wave of European revolutions that ended the Orleans monarchy – which lasted just 18 years – and led to the French Second Republic. Louis-Philippe was overthrown in February 1848 and life in the French capital began to become dangerous for intellectuals like Clovis and Aline, the daughter of socialist leader Flora Tristan. Just a little over two weeks after Gauguin's birth, the people of Paris rose in insurrection, culminating in the June days, a bloody

rebellion by workers. With peasant support, Louis Napoleon was elected president of the Second Republic. This would lead to the establishment of the Second French Empire in 1851, which would last another 20 years.

Aline Gauguin was half Peruvian, so when the revolutionaries took hold of the city in 1851 and life became increasingly hostile due to Clovis's liberalist ideals, the family left Paris bound for Peru. This hard decision was to end in a voyage to the "new world" where Aline was left to bring up her family alone: Clovis Gauguin suffered a heart attack during the journey and died. He was just 35 years old. When Aline Gauguin arrived with Paul and his older sister Marie in Peru, they settled in Lima for four years, staying with her grandfather's brother, Don Pio de Tristan Moscoso. Here, as a child, Gauguin was exposed to a simple way of life in an exotic paradise. It was a theme and influence that was to reoccur in his later life when he traveled to the South Pacific. The two Gauguin children enjoyed an affluent lifestyle, with servants, in an exotic, colorful land surrounded by racial diversity, cradled in a family with immense political power. This all changed suddenly in 1857 when civil war broke out and Aline's family lost their power. It meant a return to France for the young family, who had no choice but to move in with Clovis's brother in Orléans, where Paul attended school as a boarder when his mother found work as a dressmaker in Paris. Aline was assured of a legacy from Don Pio, who eventually left her a large annuity. Unfortunately, the family in Peru prevented Aline from ever receiving any of this money and the family lived in abject poverty.

Gauguin joined the merchant marine at the age of 17 and in 1865 he left Le Havre for Rio. He spent two years in the merchant marine before enrolling in the French Navy. Gauguin's time in the navy coincided with his mother's friendship with a wealthy neighbor and businessman, Gustave Arosa, who was given legal guardianship of her children when Aline died in 1867. Four years later, Arosa introduced Gauguin to Mette Sophie Gad and also found him work as a stockbroker when he was released from his naval obligations, having decided it was not a life he desired. Paul Gauguin and Dane, Mette Sophie Gad, were married two years later in 1873.

It was Gustave Arosa's collections of paintings by the likes of Jean-François Millet, Eugène Delacroix, and Camille Corot that were to pique Gauguin's interest in art. At the same time, his job at the stockbroker's firm introduced him to a fellow budding artist called Émile Schuffenecker. It led to artistic collaborations and Gauguin working at a local studio where he drew from a model. He also gained some lessons and, in 1876, his *Landscape at Viroflay* was accepted for the official French Salon's exhibition. He was fascinated by the works of others and for five years (between 1876 and 1881) collected a number of paintings by Camille Pissarro, former mentor to Cézanne, Monet, Manet, and Johan Barthold Jongkind. But, by the following year, Gauguin was to be affected by the financial crises that hit Paris in 1882 and resulted in him losing his comfortable job. It was at this point, encouraged by Schuffenecker, that he decided to become a full-time artist. He was unable to stay in Paris, due to financial constraints, and opted to join Pissarro in Rouen where he spent a year developing his style. By now, Gauguin

(Mary Evans Picture Library)

■ **ABOVE: French artist Ferdinand Victor Eugène Delacroix (1798-1863), one of Gauguin's early inspirations.**

■ **OPPOSITE: Painters Camille Pissarro (1830-1903) and Paul Cézanne (1839-1906), probably in Pontoise (near Paris).**

(Mary Evans/Epic/PVDE)

14

(Mary Evans/Epic/Tallandier)

■ OPPOSITE: Gauguin, shown here with his palette and brush c. 1900.

and Mette had five children. The financial pressures had seen Gauguin's wife return to her native Denmark where she worked as a translator and French teacher in Copenhagen in order to make ends meet. Living with relatives, the family just about survived, despite the lack of input from Gauguin himself. Having decided to dedicate his life to his art, Gauguin no longer had the money to support his large family and he very rarely visited them either. Émile Gauguin, the oldest of the couple's children, was born a year after their marriage, in 1874. He became an engineer, but was as fascinated by travel as his father. He had a real interest in the family's Spanish heritage and went to Colombia where he worked as a construction engineer. He married and had a son who went on to become a skilled aviator during the First World War (1914-1918). The family moved to the UK and Émile married for the second time. During the Second World War (1939-1945), he took his family to Florida, where he remained until his death in 1955.

Aline Gauguin, named after her paternal grandmother, was born in 1877 and was one of Gauguin's favorites. She died of pneumonia at the age of 20 in 1897. Likewise, her brother Clovis, named for his paternal grandfather, was another favorite. His short life – 1879 to 1900 – was cut short when he died of blood poisoning following a routine operation.

Jean René Gauguin (1881-1961) was just three years old when he moved with his mother to Denmark. He would remain here for the rest of his life, having established himself as a great artist. The youngest of the five legitimate Gauguin children was Paul Rollon "Pola" Gauguin, born in 1883. Like his older brother Jean, Pola became an artist and writer. His book, *My Father, Paul Gauguin*, is a particularly important historical manuscript.

Gauguin continued to face financial difficulties, and in 1886, having moved around a great deal, he changed from painting to ceramics for a time. The stress and worry and the fact he had lost his family – he once admitted that he had sacrificed his family for his art – saw him become gravely ill. He was hospitalized for a month and he dreamed of a simple, primitive paradise. With this in mind he left France to join his brother-in-law in Panama in April 1887, but was met with more poverty and ill health. With no money he had no choice but to work as a deck hand in order to earn his passage back to France. He brought 12 vibrantly-colored paintings with him and worked in the style of the Impressionists. It was to be a

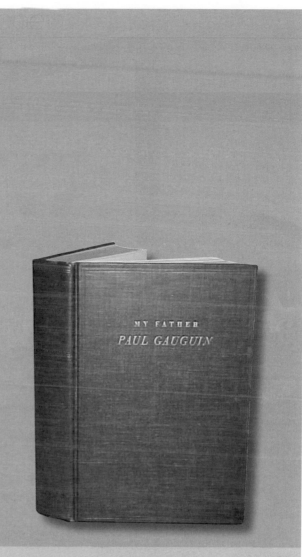

■ ABOVE: *My Father, Paul Gauguin* by Paul Rollon "Pola" Gauguin, born in 1883.

15

(Mary Evans Picture Library)

■ **ABOVE:** A Breton woman in traditional dress. Figures like this influenced Gauguin's work.

■ **OPPOSITE:** Paul Gauguin suffered with ill health but eventually recovered and returned to France.

■ **BELOW:** An exhibition poster for the Café des Arts.

GROUPE IMPRESSIONNISTE ET SYNTHÉTISTE
CAFÉ DES ARTS
VOLPINI, DIRECTEUR
EXPOSITION UNIVERSELLE
Champ-de-Mars, en face le Pavillon de la Presse

EXPOSITION DE PEINTURES
DE

Paul Gauguin	Émile Schuffenecker	Émile Bernard
Charles Laval	Louis Anquetin	Louis Roy
Léon Fauché	Daniel	Nemo

Affiche pour l'intérieur

(Public Domain)

turning point for Gauguin who, in February 1888, traveled back to Brittany, where he painted many of his great works, drawing on inspiration from the rural countryside and the Breton women whose traditional dress fascinated him.

As winter turned to spring Gauguin's health began to improve, but his work lacked his own style and direction. It was to be his subsequent meeting with Bernard that would change his course forever. Bernard introduced him to Cloisonnism, where the belief that geometry – the shapes of which all things in existence are believed to be created by – and the bright, vivid colors that accompanied the bold outlines, could further the emotional state and expression of a painting, rather than painting nature in all its reality. Gauguin followed in Bernard's style of *Breton Women in the Meadow* with his own subject, *Vision after the Sermon*. However, Gauguin's masterpiece was more realistic in its portrayal of the Breton women and perhaps far more emotive. It was Theo Van Gogh – who was acting as Gauguin's art dealer – who persuaded him to join his brother Vincent in Arles in the south of France. Wanting to escape the bad weather of another impending winter and feeling that he owed Theo Van Gogh a debt of gratitude for believing in his work, and for his support, Gauguin felt he had little choice but to join Van Gogh at his Studio of the South. It was a tumultuous nine weeks in which the two men worked side by side, but there was always an edge. Van Gogh's mental health was seriously on the decline – not for the first time – and would result in another spell in hospital for the Dutch painter. For his part, Gauguin was critical of his friend's works, which undoubtedly added to the tension and imminent ill health of Van Gogh, and yet, while there was wrangling and difficulties, he managed to produce some of his most serene pieces of the Arles countryside. Following the heated argument, where Van Gogh threatened Gauguin with a knife and then cut off part of his own ear, the French Post-Impressionist quickly returned to Paris where he found himself unable to paint very much at all. The official Paris Salon was still rejecting works in the Post-Impressionist style for their major exhibitions. As a result, Gauguin and other "modernist" painters were given permission to exhibit their works in the Café des Arts.

It was around this time that Gauguin began to add to his own collection of photographs of Buddhism and other cultures. He traveled back to Brittany while waiting to make a trip to Tonkin, in French Indo-China, where he settled for a time in Le Pouldu and painted on the walls – as was allowed – of the inn where he resided. In 1891, he made his first voyage to Tahiti in the South Pacific, where he found that French colonization and the arrival of

BAY OF PAPIETE, TAHITI —

(A SKETCH BY COUNT POUGET.)

■ **ΛBOVE:** Gauguin traveled to Tahiti where he settled and "married" a local girl, Tehamana.

(Mary Evans/Interfoto Agentur)

■ **ABOVE:** *Houses at Le Pouldu* (1890), oil on canvas.

■ **OPPOSITE:** Paul Gauguin's grave. He died at the age of 54.

missionaries dispelled his expectations of paradise from the outset. Traditional mythology – of which Gauguin had dreamed – was fast fading as "new" religion, in the form of Christianity, was gaining in momentum. He was extremely disappointed to find that what he thought existed was, in fact, no longer reality. Undeterred Gauguin continued in his quest for a primitive paradise surrounded by legend and Polynesian mythology. The year that Gauguin arrived in the South Pacific was the year his daughter, Germaine Huais (Germaine Chardon), was born to his mistress Juliette Huais, a seamstress in Paris. Germaine would go on to become a recognized artist and sculptress.

Gauguin chose, eventually, to settle in the small village of Mataiea on the south coast of Tahiti, where he became acquainted with the local chief, Tetuanui. It was Tetuanui that provided the stories of Tahitian culture that would inspire Gauguin to continue in his development of mythological art, and he often gave his works Tahitian titles, much to the annoyance of his European audiences. He "married" a local girl, Tehamana (known as Tehura), who was just 13 years old at the time. It was the relationship with this Tahitian child that would also greatly influence his works, although he was prone to introducing elements from other cultures, including idols, which didn't exist in Tahitian traditions.

His return to France in 1893 brought him little attention, except for the scandalous affair he was having with a minor, and he went back to Tahiti in 1895. Here he found a renewed energy, which culminated in a calm and quiet period for Gauguin. It was at this point that some of his greatest works were achieved. In 1899, he fathered a son with Tehura called Emile Gauguin (also known as Emile Marae a Tai), who also became an artist.

Gauguin settled in Punaauia until the fall of 1901.

From here he left for Hiva Oa, in the Marquesas Islands of French Polynesia, looking for an even simpler and cheaper existence. However, by this time, the artist had contracted syphilis, which was greatly restricting his mobility, and was also suffering from an unhealed injury.

In 1903, Gauguin made trouble by siding with the locals against the French colonists and was accused and charged with libel against the island governor, Guicheray. He was ordered to prepare his defense with three days' notice. It was the end of March 1903, but Gauguin was too ill and weak to prepare adequately and was fined 500 francs and given three months in prison. He appealed the conviction, which saw the fine remain, however, the custodial sentence was reduced to one month. But, on May 8, 1903, Gauguin died of a morphine overdose the day before he was due to start his sentence. This great man of Post-Impressionism was buried at Calvary Cemetery on Hiva Oa on the afternoon of May 9. He was just 54 years old.

Despite the reluctance to recognize Gauguin as a true genius during his lifetime, the interest in his paintings and sculptures gained rapid momentum soon after his death. Sergei Shchukin, a Russian collector, helped establish Gauguin by acquiring many of his works, (numerous works are housed in the Pushkin Museum, Moscow). And exhibitions after his death, including the exceptional exhibits organized by Fry in 1910, further ensured his legacy. Pablo Picasso was highly influenced by Gauguin, as were the French avant-garde painters and sculptors. There was a huge explosion of interest in nudes and monumental figures. Today it is rare to find an original Gauguin on the market – they are treasured and long-time held pieces that, should they find their way to an open auction, would undoubtedly sell for millions of dollars.

21

(Public Domain)

Great Works

Paintings

A Vase of Flowers

(1896)

• Oil on canvas, 25.2 in x 29.1 in (64 cm x 74 cm)

Gauguin, Paul (1848-1903); A Vase of Flowers, 1896. London, National Gallery. Oil on canvas, 64 x 74 cm. Bought, 1918. Acc.n.:1780. © 2013.
Copyright The National Gallery, London/Scala, Florence

Although many artists faced critical observation for their still life pieces, and flowers were considered outdated in terms of subject by the late 19th century, it did not deter them. Edgar Degas and Van Gogh were particularly interested in flowers for their works, the latter of whom is particularly remembered for his *Sunflowers* and *Irises* pieces. Van Gogh, in fact, would include the various stages of decay in his own floral still life works. Gauguin was associated with both artists and Degas was an early admirer who bought this piece through Daniel de Monfried in 1898. It was composed during Gauguin's final move to Tahiti, showing a vase whose color is balanced to left, right, and back, with exotic flowers, and decorated with a gold and black symmetrical cross design. Pink and red blossoms have fallen onto the muted table top, which blends with the tonal background.

And The Gold Of Their Bodies

(1901)

• Oil on canvas, 26.4 in x 29.9 in (67 cm x 76 cm)

Gauguin, Paul (1848-1903): And The Gold of Their Bodies. Paris, Musee d'Orsay. © 2013. Photo Scala, Florence

This bold painting was composed in 1901, toward the end of Gauguin's life, while in Dominica. He had sold his Tahitian property, looking for a better and cheaper way of living – that elusive Eden – although by this time he had some regular financial support from Europe. He arrived in Atuona, on the island of Hiva Oa, in the middle of September, where he purchased some land and built himself a hut. He was pleased with the move and the models, who he found gave him a sense of reinvigoration. This masterpiece shows the beauty and vulnerability of the local young women, but conveys boldness, with monumental figures against an exotic backdrop. Gauguin may have felt he had arrived in paradise, but his health began to suffer and he had to face the wrath of the authorities over the beliefs he cared to voice.

Breton Peasant Women
(1894)

• Oil on canvas, 26 in x 36.4 in (66 cm x 92.5 cm)

Gauguin, Paul (1848-1903): Paysannes Bretonnes, 1894. Paris, Musée d'Orsay. Peinture. Dim: 0.66 x 0.92m. © 2013. White Images/Scala, Florence

This stunning portrayal of Breton life combines the elements that Gauguin had come to express in his Tahitian works with the rural subjects that had inspired his earlier works. The two women chatting in the wheat field are heavily outlined – as were his later nudes – and show the overlarge feet – also a trait from these works – against a busy background of buildings, trees, a man working the land, and two other women walking away from the scene. Apart from the trees, the work shows the Cloisonnism that Gauguin and his peers had developed, and helps to bring greater "life" to the piece through the use of bright colors: the dominant reds, greens, blues, and yellows, which were also present in his French Polynesia paintings. It is perhaps obvious from his Breton works that Gauguin couldn't wait to return to Tahiti. There is, however, some ambiguity in the perspective of the work.

This is a true representation of Gauguin's Synthetism, with its emphasis on painting from memory and artistic interpretation. The work is tranquil, yet it's clear that all the subjects are actually busy. It does not convey the tempestuous state of the artist at this time. Having returned from Tahiti, Gauguin once again stayed in Le Pouldu, where the local innkeeper, Marie Meyer, refused to hand over the paintings he had previously entrusted to her. She claimed them for unpaid lodgings. He was then viciously beaten and his leg badly broken by a group of sailors in Concarneau. Two months later, his companion, Annah, left him to return to Paris where she sold all his belongings – she did, however, leave his paintings. It was an emotional time for the artist, who painted very little during 1894 – this is one of the few works he did compose.

Christ in the Garden of Olives

(1889)

• Oil on canvas, 28.7 in x 36.2 in (73 cm x 92 cm)

This is perhaps one of Gauguin's most famous religious paintings. *Christ in the Garden of Olives* shows the representation of Christ with vivid orange hair, while his disciples seem to be retreating rather than remaining with him. It is a clear depiction of storytelling, with a twist, on the night that Christ was betrayed by Judas Iscariot. The tragic figure is monumental within the piece and is, in fact, the artist himself (see the facial features). Many believe that he painted the work in this way to tell the story of his unfortunate falling out with Van Gogh (who himself had red hair). The drooping weary olive trees echo the posture of Christ and mirror the feelings of Gauguin himself, who was filled with pain after the debacle with his close friend.

Day of the Gods (Mahana No Atua)
(1894)

• Oil on canvas, 26.9 in x 36 in (68.3 cm x 91.5 cm)

The day of God, 1894, by Paul Gauguin (1848-1903). Chicago (IL), Art Institute of Chicago © 2013. DeAgostini Picture Library/Scala, Florence

This vivid painting, an imaginative interpretation of Polynesian mythology, was produced three years after Gauguin first arrived in Tahiti looking for respite, calm, and a reawakening. He returned to France in 1893, where he set about promoting his fictional work, *Noa Noa*, and this particular painting is closely related. The work is split into three horizontal sections. In the foreground, the piece concentrates on vivid, reflective hues. The middle section comprises pink sand on which symmetrical figures are placed – some suggest – to represent birth, life, and death. Their poses are mirrored in the main figure's headdress. The top section of the painting is focused on a ritual, with a monumental figure that Gauguin based on photographs from the Buddhist Temple at Borobudur in Java. The figure represents Taaroa, the creator of the world. The women to the left bring Taaroa honor gifts, while the two women on the right perform a ritual dance. The Tahitian landscape by the sea is renowned for having influenced a large number of 20th-century abstract artists.

Four Breton Girls

(1886)

• Oil on canvas, 28.3 in x 36 in (71.8 cm x 91.4 cm)

Gauguin, Paul (1848-1903): Breton Peasants, 1886. Munich, Neue Pinakothek Muenchen, Bayerische Staatsgemaeldesammlungen. Oil on canvas, 71.8 x 91.4 cm. Inv.: 8701.
© 2013. Photo Scala, Florence/BPK, Bildagentur fuer Kunst, Kultur und Geschichte, Berlin

At first glance, there does not seem to be a particular story in this painting. It shows four Breton girls in a field with no particular purpose other than they exist. The background points to the artist's Impressionist roots, but the subject suggests a more symbolic approach – a nod to deeper meanings hidden in reality – showing a subject not immediately visible. The girls seem to take on a dance-like formation, where each is given as much interest and equality as the others. The three figures in the foreground are clearly formed and their dresses are clearly flowing; the fourth figure, to the back with red hair, is more obscured, perhaps a more blatant move to hide behind reality. However, the figure to the right is leaning on the hay bale, which clearly obscures the girl behind it, while fixing her shoe. The painting consists of a natural landscape, but color is evident alongside patterns that highlight this rustic scene.

Hail Mary (La Orana Maria)

(1891)

• Oil on canvas, 44.8 in x 34.5 in (113.7 cm x 87.6 cm)

Gauguin, Paul (1848-1903): Ia Orana Maria (Hail Mary), 1891. New York, Metropolitan Museum of Art. Oil on canvas, 44 3/4 x 34 1/2 in. (113.7 x 87.6 cm). Inscribed: Signed, dated, and inscribed: (lower right) P. Gauguin 91; (lower left) IA ORANA MARIA (HailMary). Bequest of Sam A. Lewisohn, 1951. Acc.n.: 51.112.2. © 2013. Image copyright The Metropolitan Museum of Art/ArtResource/Scala, Florence

Gauguin produced this, his first major Tahitian canvas – although he would later compose a series of Polynesian-inspired religious belief paintings – and revealed both Mary and Jesus to his audience. They were depicted as Tahitians, who are introduced by an angel with yellow wings. Gauguin was particularly happy with this piece, which he painted with a somber background of mountains and exotic foliage. However, in the vivid green foreground, he also paints bananas and other exotic fruit placed in a leaf-shaped bowl on a small table, as if they are offerings on an altar. The composition was based on a photograph that the artist had of Borobudur, the Buddhist Temple in Java. The halos over Mary and the naked boy, Jesus, clearly show Gauguin's religious beliefs, but the audience could be forgiven, if these were not easily identified at first glance, for thinking that this was a further interpretation of naked Tahitian women. The two Maori women approaching the Madonna and child are depicted wearing the traditional *pareus*, a draped cloth worn from the waist, which cleverly combines the Polynesian themes with Westernized influences – note the hands held together in symbolic prayer. In reality, however, Tahitian women at this time were dressed modestly – in dresses provided by missionaries. Gauguin was also radical in his approach to the Madonna and child by painting them as Tahitians. Western art had only ever contained white depictions of Mary and Jesus, and Papal consent to include other portrayals was not actually given until 1951.

Gauguin used poetic license as an artist to compose this work, with its monumental figures, and intended for it to portray timelessness, uncluttered by the end of the 19th century's modern culture. The painting is spontaneous and colorful, if somewhat contradictory. Gauguin reveled in the "primitive" life he found and admired in Polynesia, yet chose to represent it with Westernized beliefs – the very same as those he was trying to escape.

Joyousness (Arearea)

(1892)

- Oil on canvas, 29.5 in x 37 in (75 cm x 94 cm)

Gauguin, Paul (1848-1903): Arearea, 1892. Paris, Musee d'Orsay. Oil on canvas, 75 x 94 cm.© 2013. Photo Scala, Florence

Arearea represents a place where dreams and reality exist side by side. The background sky, painted in dark tones of blue and black, is almost obscured in this composition of red, green, and yellow color planes. The painting was one of a series of works from this time that Gauguin included in a collection for an exhibition in Paris in 1893. It was the artist's way of hoping to garner favor for his first exotic foray to the South Pacific. He was sorely disappointed that he did not receive the enthusiasm for the exhibition he had hoped for; the red dog received scathing remarks, while the titles in Tahitian did little to persuade the critics and public that Gauguin had achieved something remarkable. Undeterred, Gauguin was convinced that *Joyousness* was one of his greatest paintings, in which he depicts a huge Buddha and a sacred rite in the background. The foreground is focused on motifs – that occur throughout his paintings at this time. A large, sparse, but solid tree cuts across the piece and dominates to the right, under which sit two women, alongside the red dog. It was Gauguin's interpretation of an idealized Polynesia, with worldly men and gods who provided the protection in this enchanted land.

Landscape

(1873)

• Oil on canvas, 19.9 in x 32.1 in (50.5 cm x 81.6 cm)

Landscape, 1873, by Paul Gauguin (1848-1903). Cambridge, Fitzwilliam Museum. © 2013. DeAgostini Picture Library/Scala, Florence

Composed in 1873, Gauguin painted *Landscape* during his spare time, away from his work as a stockbroker. He was persuaded by Pissarro and Degas to take part in the fourth Impressionist exhibition in 1879. (He previously exhibited in 1876.) This elongated landscape is reminiscent of Pissarro, whom he admired, and contains warm earthy tones that contrast in balance with the brightness of the sky and clouds. It is a rustic, rural scene with diagonal and horizontal planes. Some experts question the perspective of the painting, but the eye is perhaps drawn by the tree and foliage on the left before being steered toward the center of the piece and the faraway background and land beyond.

- Oil on canvas, 36 in x 28.5 in (91.4 cm x 72.5 cm)

Landscape in Brittany, 1888 (1939). Found in the collection of the Indianapolis Museum of Art. Plate taken from "Gauguin," by John Rewald, published by William Heinemann (London and Toronto, printed in France and Belgium, 1939). London, The Print Collector. © 2013. Photo The Print Collector/Heritage-Images/Scala, Florence

This painting is exquisite in its vivid landscape of Arles and the central geometric haystack. It was the first work that Gauguin produced at the Studio of the South. Looking at this painting, it would not be immediately obvious that the artist was suffering emotional turmoil during a difficult two-month stay with his close friend, Van Gogh. The relationship between the two men was "charged." This is perhaps apparent in the brooding sky above the scene and the movement of the tallest tree. However, it is widely accepted that Van Gogh's emotional outbursts toward his friend affected Gauguin the "man" rather than Gauguin the "artist." Gauguin's art was more likely to be influenced by Cézanne – who did not return the favor – rather than Vincent Van Gogh. Perhaps this influence can be seen in this painting, with its cubic structure of verticals mixed with horizontals through distinct planes: walls and houses. There are also diagonals, but the distant hills, the blue hues of the trees, and the vibrant orange of the roof tiles all point to Cézanne. However, the broken colors – note the haystack – and the foreground are more reminiscent of Van Gogh. It shows that without the need to copy the work of others Gauguin had a clear perception of the fundamental elements and techniques of the paintings of his peers. The work was produced after a summer spent in Pont-Aven, at a time when he rejected and moved on from Impressionism. The piece is important in terms of the artist's focus on structure and forms, and he emphasizes the geometrics of the piece – in the style of Cézanne. For Van Gogh, Gauguin's two months in Provence was the only time that he came anywhere close to realizing his dream of the Studio of the South. It was surely short-lived.

Les Alyscamps

(1888)

• Oil on canvas, 36 in x 28.5 in (91.5 cm x 72.5 cm)

Gauguin, Paul (1848-1903): Les Alyscamps. Paris, Musee d'Orsay. © 2013. Photo Scala, Florence

Gauguin arrived at the Studio of the South in October 1888. He was the only peer of Van Gogh's that had agreed to give the concept of an artist "brotherhood" a try. Gauguin and Van Gogh had been writing to each other for several months prior to the fall of 1888. Each had been experimenting with creating a non-naturalist landscape. When Gauguin arrived in Arles he was fairly quick to compose *Les Alyscamps,* with its colors of the fall in all their flaming glory against the backdrop of the Roman Necropolis, consecrated in the 3rd century by Saint Trophime as a burial ground, and the canal. Although by the 19th century little remained of the site apart from a few sarcophagi (none of which are present here) and the avenues of poplar trees, the scene conjured by Gauguin is rich and diverse. In this piece the artist incorporates the church of St. Honorat, although he leaves out all other historical references and includes the figures of one man and two Arlesiennes women. He portrays the canal and vegetation, and the canvas as a whole, using the brushstrokes of Cézanne and characteristics of his own Synthetism. Gauguin's interpretation of the scene, with its hatching and subjective vision, is somewhat different to the tormented versions by Van Gogh.

Gauguin had arrived in Arles with financial support from Theo Van Gogh. He is known to have said he was less impressed with the burial site than his friend, but he does nod to the railway workshops just across the canal through the inclusion of steam train smoke in the top left of the work. He also pays homage to the Arlesiennes and the fact that the site was a popular place to walk, especially for lovers. The canal appears to divide the work in two: the left side of the painting is cool and focuses on the vegetation, smoke, and sky, while the right side is given over to vibrant colors of fall in the trees, in orange and yellow hues.

Night Café at Arles

(1888)

• Oil on canvas, 28.3 in x 36.2 in (72 cm x 92 cm)

Gauguin, Paul (1848-1903): At the Café or Café in Arles (Mme. Ginoux). Moscow, Pushkin Museum. © 2013. Photo Scala, Florence

Unlike Van Gogh's vision of drinkers who are isolated and alone, Gauguin tackles the same subject in *Night Café at Arles* in a much more upbeat and approachable way. He does not compose his drinkers as loners but as figures rejoicing in being together, resided over by the café owner, Madame Ginoux, represented here in the foreground (like a portraiture) as the dominant figure, seated with blue carafe. She appears all seeing and all knowing in the piece that contains contrasting scenes and Gauguin's Cloisonnism in horizontal lines across the canvas. Madame Ginoux also posed for Van Gogh, who took three nights to complete his work.

Nirvana: Portrait of Meyer de Haan

(c. 1889-1890)

• Gouache on cotton, 8.7 in x 11.2 in (22 cm x 28.5 cm)

Gauguin, Paul (1848-1903): Nirvana: Portrait of Meyer de Haan, c. 1889-90. Hartford (CT), Wadsworth Atheneum Museum of Art. Gouache on cotton, 8 x 11 1/2 in. The Ella Gallup Sumner and Mary Catlin Sumner Collection Fund. 1943.445. © 2013. Wadsworth Atheneum Museum of Art /Art Resource, NY/Scala, Florence

This painting depicts Gauguin's friend, Jacob Meyer de Haan, as the devil holding a snake that has formed the letter "G" with its writhing body. Behind the devil are two female nudes who represent life and death. They lie seductively behind the devil, while the foreground clearly shows the word "Nirvana." The painting pays homage to his friend while at the same time ridiculing him in its depiction. The two men had stayed at Le Pouldu in Pont-Aven, where de Haan had fathered a daughter. Gauguin and de Haan shared an emotionally-charged relationship.

Old Women of Arles

(1888)

• Oil on canvas, 28.7 in x 36.2 in (73 cm x 92 cm)

Gauguin was critical of Van Gogh's work, particularly regarding the speed with which his friend worked. It led to Van Gogh becoming confused. Gauguin preferred to paint from imagination and to conjure his own interpretations. He felt that Van Gogh relied far more heavily on nature than was necessary. Gauguin, like Cézanne, was a slow and deliberate artist, careful to work and rework his paintings until he had developed a sustainable pictorial harmony, often with symbolic content. *Old Women of Arles* is particularly faithful to these ideals. The painting, however, is rather ambiguous. It is a flat portrayal of women who are almost placed to the left of the work to form a pyramid, perhaps mirroring the straw coverings over the plants to the right, but it is unclear as to whether the audience is supposed to realize what the coverings are. If you look closely at the large green bush in the foreground, to the left of the gate, you can just make out a face – some commentators have also questioned whether this was intended. And, if so, why?

Another interesting observation is that the two closer women cover their mouths and avoid the audience, while the two women further behind seem to look directly out of the painting. This was another early work that Gauguin composed in his first few weeks at Arles, but it is not particularly clear what the story here is trying to convey. It is perhaps possible that Gauguin was depicting the garden in a very different way to the versions that Van Gogh created – maybe in a reaction to his friend's works. Whatever the reason for the hidden messages and the painting's ambiguity, it is a beautiful, if somewhat disturbing, interpretation of a "common" scene.

Schuffenecker's Studio

(1889)

• Oil on canvas, 28.7 in x 36.2 in (73 cm x 92 cm)

Gauguin, Paul (1848-1903): Schuffenecker's Studio. Paris, Musee d'Orsay. © 2013. Photo Scala, Florence

Gauguin, despite sharing a friendship with stockbroker employee and amateur painter Émile Schuffenecker for nearly 20 years, found it difficult not to reveal his contempt for the man. In this work, *Schuffenecker's Studio*, that contempt is clear. However, Schuffenecker had shown a great deal of support for Gauguin and had been instrumental in the artist's decision to take up painting full time. The work shows Van Gogh's influence, in the primary contrasting colors, and he treats the Schuffenecker children with sensitivity. He is less sensitive when it comes to Émile and his wife Louise – she was known to have been indifferent to Gauguin, and it was rumored that he had tried to seduce her to no avail – here she is shown as dominant and demanding, while he is rather cruel to Émile. The figure has no paintbrush, thereby being denied his status as a painter, and he looks meek as a husband.

Still Life with Fruit and Lemons

(c. 1880)

• Oil on canvas, 19.7 in x 24 in (50 cm x 61 cm)

Still Life with Fruit, Brittany, 19th century (1939). Plate taken from "Gauguin", by John Rewald, published by William Heinemann (London and Toronto, printed in France and Belgium, 1939). London, The Print Collector. © 2013. Photo The Print Collector/Heritage-Images/Scala, Florence

This beautiful painting was created while Gauguin still had a full-time job as a stockbroker. It shows the technical potential he would come to master. Obviously, it portrays his early influences in Impressionism – with the still life subject – and is fairly reminiscent of Cézanne. The influence of using color is also evident and perhaps a sign of what was to come in later works.

Still Life with Three Puppies

(1888)

• Oil on wood, 36.1 in x 24.6 in (91.8 cm x 62.6 cm)

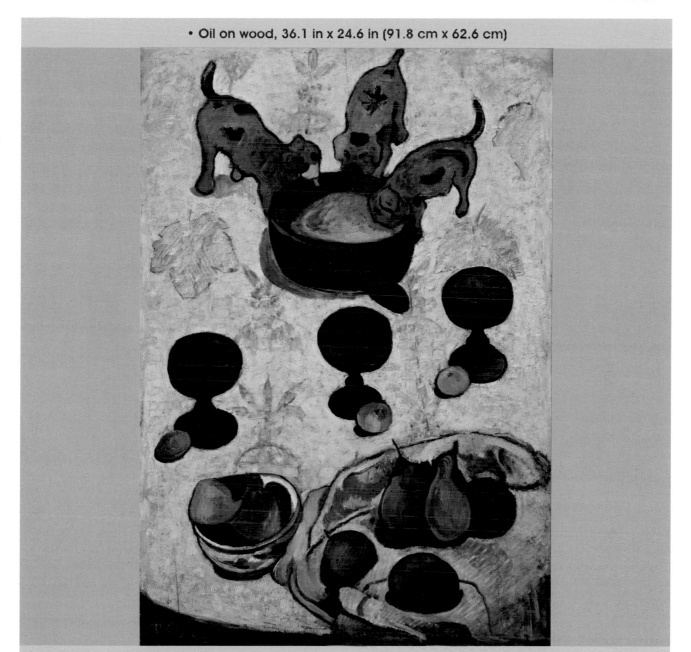

Gauguin, Paul (1848-1903). Still Life with Three Puppies, 1888. New York, Museum of Modern Art (MoMA). Oil on wood, 36 1/8 x 24 5/8 in. (91.8 x 62.6 cm). Mrs. Simon Guggenheim Fund. Acc. n.:48.1952. © 2013. Digital image, The Museum of Modern Art, New York/Scala, Florence

This work has three elements, or subjects, including the three tri-colored puppies drinking from a large pan, three blue glasses, each accompanied by a piece of fruit, which diagonally separate the dogs from the still life elements in the foreground. By the time Gauguin composed this piece he was living in Brittany and experimenting with color. Notice how the puppies are outlined in blue rather than natural tones and hues. Commentaries state that Gauguin drew inspiration for the work from Japanese prints, which Van Gogh introduced him to in 1888. It was a time of abandonment and experimentation and shows that he was working toward painting in a style that was not yet realized or understood. There is no reality in the perspective, yet the work is balanced. The outlines are exaggerated and bold, and shadows are overlooked. In his letters from the time, Gauguin often mentioned "abstract" works and a new form of freedom from both reality and nature. It could be seen as a painting (in terms of its treatment of planes, colors, abstract nature, and lack of shadows and perspectives) ahead of its time.

Study of a Nude
(1880)

• Oil on canvas, 43.9 in x 31.3 in (111.4 cm x 79.5 cm)

Study of a Nude, 1880. Artist: Paul Gauguin From the collection of the Glyptothek Museum, Copenhagen, Denmark. © 2013. Photo Art Media/Heritage Images/Scala, Florence

This early painting shows painstaking work of a nude who, while dominating her surroundings, fits perfectly within them. The fact that the figure is sewing – while wearing nothing at all – is interesting. The painting is an honest and realistic interpretation of the figure. However, as Gauguin's style and techniques developed, reality would become less and less important.

Tahitian Women on the Beach

(1891)

• Oil on canvas, 27.2 in x 36 in (69 cm x 91.5 cm)

Tahitian Women on the Beach, 1891 (1939). Found in the collection of the Musee d'Orsay, Paris, France. Plate taken from "Gauguin," by John Rewald, published by William Heinemann (London and Toronto, printed in France and Belgium, 1939). London, The Print Collector. © 2013. Photo The Print Collector/Heritage-Images/Scala, Florence

This exquisite work shows Gauguin's penchant for large feet and hands – commonplace in his works of Tahitians. When he first arrived in Tahiti he was expecting a land of primitive culture set within a timeless paradise. He was hoping that traveling to an exotic clime would set him free. Here he depicts two women, one of who is busy with a daily task, in a confident and bold work. The sea – to the top of the painting – works in harmony with the sand where the women dominate the middle and foreground in vibrant colors. The simply portrayed women appear close, yet lost in their own thoughts – a common occurrence in Gauguin's "group" paintings.

The Beautiful Angèle (La Belle Angèle)
(1889)

• Oil on canvas, 36.2 in x 28.7 in (92 cm x 73 cm)

LA BELLE ANGÈLE

Gauguin, Paul (1848-1903): La Belle Angele. Paris, Musee d'Orsay. © 2013. Photo Scala, Florence

This exciting portraiture – of which Gauguin was proud – is of Marie-Angélique Satre, who ran a guesthouse in Pont-Aven with her husband. The sitter found the piece disturbing at the time as Gauguin had moved away from traditional portraits and had experimented with spatial elements and perspective. He has framed the figure – inspired by Japanese prints – and partitioned her from the background. The sitter is fairly rigid in ceremonial costume, which reinforces the formal and solemn approach to the subject. Two years after its completion Degas bought the piece, declaring it a "masterpiece." Despite the decorative background, Gauguin is confident in his simplistic approach to the portrait.

The Moon and the Earth (Hina Te Fatou)
(1893)

- Oil on burlap, 45 in x 24.5 in (114.3 cm x 62.2 cm)

Gauguin, Paul (1848-1903): The Moon and the Earth (Hina Te Fatou), 1893. New York, Museum of Modern Art (MoMA). Oil on burlap, 45 x 24 1/2 in (114.3 x 62.2 cm). Lillie P. Bliss Collection. 50.1934. ©2013. Digital image, The Museum of Modern Art, New York/Scala, Florence

Gauguin was particularly interested in Polynesian mythology and was inspired to compose this work based on Hina (the female spirit of the moon) and Fatou (the male spirit of earth). The myth revolves around Hina asking Fatou to give man eternal life, but he refuses her request. This piece shows a naked Hina facing an oversized Fatou who can only be seen from the waist up. There is no compromise between the two – only contrasts and an unresolved story. It is not entirely clear what Gauguin intended with his portrayal of the myth, with its monumental figures set in an exotic backdrop. The darker hues surrounding these figures are interspersed with flashes of bold color.

The Poor Fisherman

(1896)

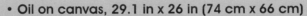

• Oil on canvas, 29.1 in x 26 in (74 cm x 66 cm)

The poor fisherman, by Paul Gauguin (1848-1903). Sao Paulo, Museu de Arte de Sao Paulo. © 2013. DeAgostini PictureLibrary/Scala, Florence

This beautiful portrayal of a poor fisherman was a Biblical reference, which Gauguin returned to a number of times. The theme speaks of a simple life, filled with poverty, of an isolated fisherman sitting in a melancholic state next to his boat. The natural hues and calmness they project add to the melancholic feel of this stunning work, and contrast brilliantly with the chaotic reds in the foreground. The background is exotic and represents a nature filled with luxury, yet the subject of the piece is clearly not living in paradise. The figure is thin and withdrawn, perhaps lost in thought. It is undoubtedly a painting of contrasts: exotic nature versus harsh impoverished reality, swirling red tones against horizontal calm background.

The Sacred Mountain (Parahi Te Marae)
(1892)

• Oil on canvas, 26 in x 35 in (66 cm x 88.9 cm)

Gauguin, Paul (1848-1903): The Sacred Mountain (Parahi Te Marae), 1892. Philadelphia, Philadelphia Museum of Art. © 2013.
Photo The Philadelphia Museum of Art/Art Resource/Scala, Florence

The painting comprises a sacred enclosure in the Marquesas Islands and the original title of the work was *There is the Marae* (meaning Temple of Prayers and Sacrifices). Like the other Tahitian paintings, this work did not receive a positive reception when it was first exhibited in Paris in 1893. This particular painting was composed from Gauguin's imagination, although he was well aware of local legends about sacrificial children. Here he depicts exotic flowers in vibrant colors leading up to the sacred enclosure which comprises a golden-yellow hill, with trees and green and orange foliage all just below a great mountain. On the hill sits a giant idol. Gauguin used hatched brushstrokes for the piece and created rounded and flattened forms. He often insisted that he was not a painter who worked from nature, and this imaginative piece demonstrates his point.

- Oil on burlap mounted on canvas, 28.5 in x 38.4 in (72.4 cm x 97.5 cm)

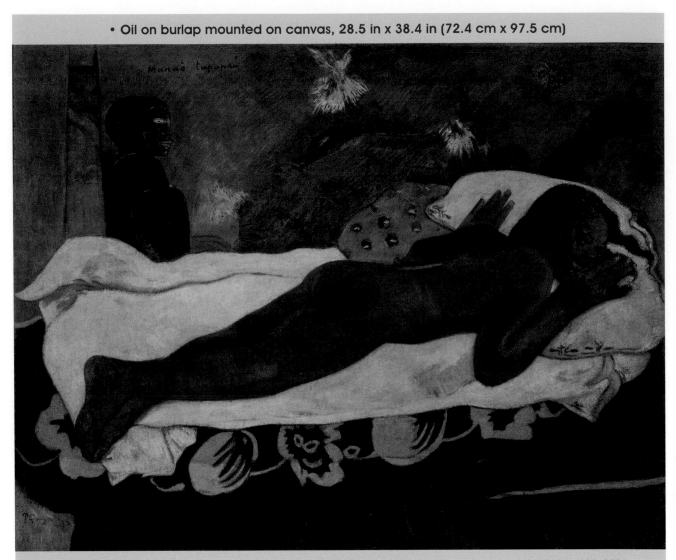

Gauguin, Paul (1848-1903): Spirit of the Dead Watching, 1892. Buffalo (NY), Albright-Knox Art Gallery. Oil on burlap mounted on canvas. Framed: 36 1/4 x 44 1/2 x 2 1/2 in (92.075 x 113.03 x 6.35cm); support: 28 1/2 x 38 3/8 i. (72.39 x 97.4725 cm). A. Conger Goodyear Collection, 1965. © 2013. Albright Knox Art Gallery/Art Resource, NY/Scala, Florence Kunst, Kultur und Geschichte, Berlin

This work was inspired by Gauguin's young Tahitian wife who, lying naked on the bed, was disturbed by her husband's arrival home and the sudden striking of a match in the darkness. Gauguin's wife is portrayed together with a spirit (known in local legends as a "watching") keeping watch over her at the end of the bed. Like many of his other works, this painting combines the ordinary with the mysterious extraordinary through a series of simplified forms in horizontal and vertical planes. It is one of Gauguin's most famous works and suggests that a supernatural world exists alongside reality in a parallel realm. Here, the naked figure is aware that she is not alone and, without wanting to appear it, is actually extremely frightened at the spirit's presence. In Gauguin's *Self-portrait with a Hat* this painting is reversed in the background.

The Swineherd

(1888)

• Oil on canvas, 28.7 in x 36.6 in (73 cm x 93 cm)

This painting is a lively, harmonious work of natural hues in the Impressionist style. The planes of the work are overlapping, and some outlines – note the swine – are vaguely defined. The left side is particularly reminiscent of the Impressionists, however, the colors indicate a modern approach and serenity between the artist and his subject. This simple scene suggests that Gauguin enjoyed and reveled in simple forms and a simple life, which he often composed in his paintings.

The White Horse

(1898)

- Oil on canvas, 55.1 in x 36 in (140 cm x 91.5 cm)

The White Horse, 1898 (1939). Found in the collection of the Musee d'Orsay, Paris, France. Plate taken from "Gauguin," by John Rewald, published by William Heinemann (London and Toronto, printed in France and Belgium, 1939). London, The Print Collector. © 2013. Photo The Print Collector/Heritage-Images/Scala, Florence

This painting was composed on Gauguin's second trip to Tahiti. He liked to object to any suggestion that he painted from nature, however, he was particularly taken with exploring the countryside. Despite this, *The White Horse* was inspired by his imagination rather than from a particular panoramic vision he stumbled across on the island. Here he depicts horses with naked, barebacked riders amongst an exotic backdrop of foliage and water. In the absence of roads and vehicles horses were the main transport on Tahiti – Gauguin had not failed to notice that everyone had sound horsemanship skills and he was keen to portray this within this painting. The main horse, without a rider, is drinking from a stream in the foreground of the piece, while the canvas is void of sky or a horizon. This animal is perhaps used to represent death and worship of the gods: the color white is associated with both in Polynesia. However, in the piece, the animal is tinged with the green of the vibrant foliage of the forest. This work has become one of Gauguin's most famous pieces, so it is interesting to note that the buyer who originally commissioned the work refused it because the horse was "too green."

The Yellow Christ

(1889)

• Oil on canvas, 36.3 in x 28.9 in (92.1 cm x 73.3 cm)

Interestingly, Gauguin sets the crucifixion of Christ in Brittany in northern France. The work is among his most famous, with its Cloisonnism (the areas are separated by bold outlines), and Symbolism. 19th-century women, in traditional dress, who have gathered at the foot of the cross, surround Christ. None of the women look at the crucified man directly, but all appear pious and melancholy with their bowed heads. Christ's eyes are closed as his yellow form sits against a background of yellows, greens, purples, and reds. This religious portrayal pays homage to the Breton women and the rural landscape in which they lived and worked. He painted a large number of scenes depicting peasant life. The artist has chosen to set the scene during the fall, at harvest time, which may be his way of linking the seasons and the circle of rural life with the cycle of Christ, that is, Crucifixion (harvest), Christ's three days in the tomb (winter), and Christ's rebirth (spring).

Two Tahitian Women

(1899)

• Oil on canvas, 37 in x 28.5 in (94 cm x 72.4 cm)

Gauguin, Paul (1848-1903): Two Tahitian Women, 1899. New York, Metropolitan Museum of Art. Oil on canvas, 37 x 28 1/2 in (94 x 72.4 cm). Inscribed: Signed and dated (lower left): 99 / PGauguin. Gift of William Church Osborn, 1949. Acc.n.: 49.58.1 © 2013. Image copyright The Metropolitan Museum of Art/Art Resource/Scala, Florence

This beautiful portrayal of Tahitian life was composed as Gauguin's stay on the island was about to end. It was at this time that he moved away from the Symbolist style and concentrated on portraitures, showing the beauty of the islanders and their relaxed attitude to the human body. This painting is a romanticized view of Tahitian life – in reality, many women wore full dresses supplied by missionaries – and a reaction to Gauguin's disappointment in the Westernized way of life. These two women were depicted in his frieze *Tahitian Pastoral* the year before he reworked the painting as *Two Tahitian Women*, and appeared again in the monumental *Rupe, Rupe*, also composed in 1899.

The painting, included in an exhibition at the National Gallery of Art in April 2011 while on loan from The Metropolitan Museum of Art in New York, was targeted by a woman. Fortunately, the work was protected by plexiglass and the woman, who had hit the protective covering and tried to pull the painting away from the wall, was unsuccessful in her attempt: she was restrained by a security officer and charged with destruction of property and attempted theft. The painting was thoroughly examined – where it was established that no damage was sustained – before being put back on display.

Vision after the Sermon (Jacob Wrestling with the Angel)
(1888)

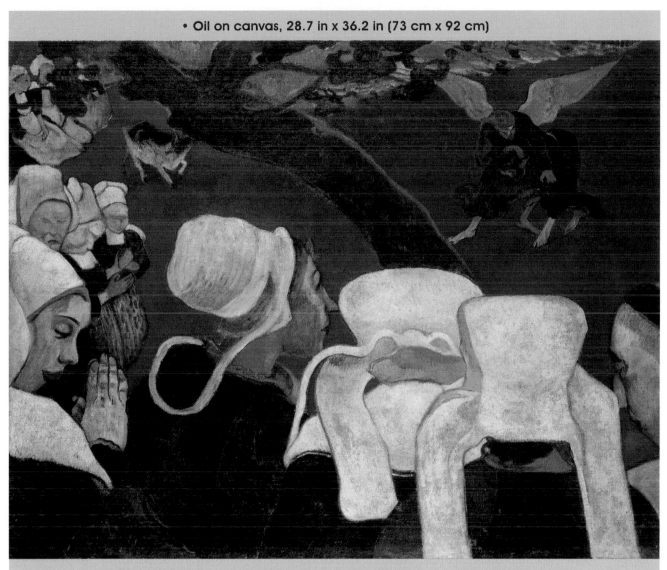

• Oil on canvas, 28.7 in x 36.2 in (73 cm x 92 cm)

The vision after the sermon, by Paul Gauguin Digital (1848-1903). Edinburgh, Scottish National Gallery. © 2013. DeAgostini Picture Library/Scala, Florence

Again, Gauguin sets his Biblical scene in Breton surroundings. It is a move away from the Impressionist subjects of rural and city landscapes to one of Breton women standing and praying while Jacob wrestles with an angel. This depiction is a modern take on the Renaissance style, with emphasized bold outlines and vibrant color. *Vision after the Sermon* is considered a Gauguin masterpiece – alongside *The Yellow Christ* – and both paintings are treated away from their historical contexts. The large tree across the center of the piece is reminiscent of Japanese woodcuts and serves to separate the pious women from the struggle between Jacob and the angel. Gauguin's fascination with rural, rustic, and the almost primitive way of life for peasants, helped to secure his influence at the Pont-Aven school.

What, Are You Jealous? (Aha oe feii?)

(1892)

Rather than suggesting that there is any rivalry between the two women depicted in this portraiture, it has been cited that the title of this work, *What, Are You Jealous?*, was intended for Gauguin's peers and critics. One woman sits dominant in the center of the piece with her naked body facing to the front, left leg crossed over right leg, while her left hand rests on her leg, her right hand steadies her posture, and her face is tilted to the left toward the woman lying behind her. The seated woman is based on a figure in a photograph of a frieze at the Theatre of Dionysus, Athens, while the white garland around her head could represent a laurel wreath. It is suggested that the second woman, lying down, was added later. Gauguin has escaped realism in this piece in his quest to use color to great effect. Note the women's discarded clothing, the pink, hot sand, and the abstract water.

Woman with a Flower

(1891)

- Oil on canvas, 27.6 in x 18.1 in (70 cm x 46 cm)

Gauguin, Paul (1848-1903): Vahine no te Tiare, 1891. © 2013. Photo Scala, Fiorence/BPK, Bildagentur fuer Kunst, Kultur und Geschichte, Berlin

Gauguin described the woman in this portrait as "beautiful," although he didn't mean as in "pretty" but rather as in strength. This is an early painting from his arrival in Tahiti, which still clearly connects with the European way of life he'd left behind: note the woman's apparel and the formal pose. However, the figure's exotic features point to a new and exciting existence, as can be seen in the bright colors and decorative background. This was the first painting that Gauguin sent "home" as a way of introducing the new subjects he'd discovered since his arrival in the South Pacific. Unfortunately, Gauguin did not receive a warm reception to his Tahitian portrait, which failed to impress. This beautiful woman is holding a single, orange flower as she stares resolutely out of the canvas, but not at the audience – she looks to a spot that we cannot see and do not know what holds her gaze. Her formal clothes of blue smock dress and stiff white collar contrast brilliantly with her cascading black hair and the vivid background.

Where Do We Come From? What Are We? Where Are We Going?

(1897)

• Oil on canvas, 54.8 in x 147.5 in (139.1 cm x 374.6 cm)

Just like the title, this work is divided into three sections. The story moves from the right to the left of the canvas, giving a response to each question posed in the title of the piece. Notice that each question is asked in the top left corner, but without question marks.

The first stage of the story relates to childhood, shown to the right with a baby lying in the immediate foreground. In the center of the piece the artist focuses on adolescence before moving on to old age and impending death on the

left side. While the painting is based on a long tradition of showing different stages of life - a Westernized ideal – it isn't a religious work, although it does nod toward a spiritual element. It is understood that this is a highly personal work, exploring the realities of the artist's own life and the way in which he viewed the world during his idealized and romanticized life in the South Pacific.

Great Works
Self-portraits

Self-portrait with a Hat

(1893-1894)

• Oil on canvas, double sided, 18.1 in x 15 in (46 cm x 38 cm)

Gauguin, Paul (1848-1903): Self-portrait. Paris, Musee d'Orsay. © 2013. Photo Scala, Florence

Self-portrait with a Hat shows the significance to the artist of the *Manao Tupapau* work in which his young Tahitian wife is lying naked on a bed, watched over by a "watching." The small version of the piece is included in this self-portrait of Gauguin in reverse, suggesting that the artist is looking in a mirror. The mirror theme is then continued with the decoration motif on the bedding (in the small version), which is copied on the sarong behind Gauguin. It is suggested that Gauguin painted this self-portrait as a response to the lackluster reviews he had received when he returned to Paris in 1893 and gave an exhibition of his Tahitian masterpieces. The backdrop to this painting is his studio in Tahiti, which he painted in yellow and olive green, while he gives himself a rather rugged and exotic look. The back of this self-portrait saw another composition, that of William Molard, a friend of Gauguin's. This was one of the works that would eventually become influential in introducing Primitivism at the beginning of the 20th century.

Self-portrait with Halo

(1889)

• Oil on panel, 31.2 in x 20.2 in (79.2 cm x 51.3 cm)

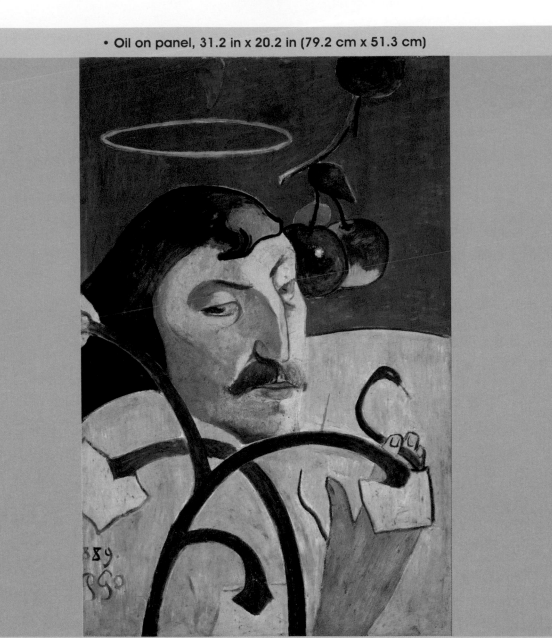

Gauguin, Paul (1848-1903): Self-portrait. Washington DC, National Gallery of Art. © 2013. DeAgostini Picture Library/Scala, Florence

This work, *Self-portrait with Halo*, is considered to be one of the most famous of Gauguin's paintings. Here, he cleverly utilizes large areas of vivid flat colors, and ensures that artists of the future will no longer be tied to the ideals of painting from nature. From this painting onward, artists would be free to approach their own works in a personalized and radical way – tradition was changing and, with this, a modern style was beginning to blossom. Gauguin, with his determination to paint in the way he wanted and needed, had turned the tables and opened up a whole new artistic vision. This self-portrait was one of many. It was created after Gauguin's less than successful time in Arles with Van Gogh and was part of a series of works that he produced while staying in Le Pouldu with de Haan. This particular piece was painted on cupboard doors at the inn where the two men were lodging. Note how the portrait is almost a caricature – opinion is divided as to whether Gauguin saw himself as the devil or Christ in this depiction. What does the halo add? What about the apples and the serpent? Is this a reflection of a fall from grace or is it the artist's intention to portray himself as a hero? The head is almost positioned as if on a platter – it's difficult to interpret the true meaning of this groundbreaking painting.

Self-portrait with Yellow Christ

(1891)

• Oil on canvas, 15 in x 18.1 in (38 cm x 46 cm)

Gauguin, Paul (1848-1903): Autoportrait au Christ jaune, 1891. Paris, Musee d'Orsay. Peinture. Dim: 0.38 x 0.46 m. © 2013. WhiteImages/Scala, Florence

This self-portrait was composed just before Gauguin's trip to Tahiti in 1891, at a time when he faced great turmoil. Alongside the portrait of himself he has included two other paintings that he created the year before. While the artist remains the dominant central protagonist *The Yellow Christ* is included to the left of the piece, while *Grotesque Head* contrasts in color to the right.

Both the earlier works were created in the artist's likeness and represent the character and personality of Gauguin which, combined with his staring self-portrait here, show a wild and vulnerable man on the brink of a new life, unsure of what that might bring. This painting uses bold colors and his trademark heavy outlines and is a clear indication that this piece is about his feelings and mood rather than being based on what Gauguin saw. This was truly revolutionary.

Gauguin
In The 21st Century

(Public Domain)

■ ABOVE: The Paul Gauguin Museum (Tahiti).

Gauguin's legacy is that he was one of the pioneers of modernism, a true inspiration from the Post-Impressionist era. Today there is huge interest in Gauguin, and while no imminent exhibitions are planned, there have been many dedicated to this monumental artist in the 21st century. There are also collections of his paintings and other works around the world, including the Paul Gauguin Museum in Tahiti. This museum is dedicated to his life and paintings, with a timeline and synopses of his great works, comprising French Polynesian and Marquesan cultural elements within the exhibits. There are photographs, documents, sculptures, engravings, and reproductions, alongside sketches and block prints. The museum actively works with other museums, galleries, and institutions to place Gauguin's works on display. It could be described as more of a monument to the artist than a museum as all the paintings are prints and posters of the originals – except where works are entrusted on loan for timely exhibitions. The Japanese-styled museum is ordered in such a way that visitors are invited to walk through a timeline of the artist's life. Despite the lack of original paintings the museum is set within beautiful grounds, with an idyllic backdrop overlooking the sea. The museum also houses the works of Tahitian artists and Constance Gordon-Cumming. In Atuona, the Paul Gauguin Cultural Center (le Centre Culturel Paul Gauguin) is home to exhibits of the artist.

Useful Websites

The Pushkin Museum of Fine Arts
12 Volkhonka Street, Moscow, Russia
www.arts-museum.ru

The State Hermitage Museum (The Hermitage)
St. Petersburg, Russia
www.hermitagemuseum.org

Metropolitan Museum of Art
1000 Fifth Avenue, New York, USA
www.metmuseum.org

Museum of Fine Arts
465 Huntington Avenue, Boston, Massachusetts, USA
www.mfa.org

Musée d'Orsay
62 rue de Lille, 75343 Paris, France
www.musee-orsay.fr

The State Hermitage Museum
2 Dvortsovaya Square, St. Petersburg, Russia
www.hermitagemuseum.org

The National Gallery
Trafalgar Square, London, UK
www.nationalgallery.org.uk

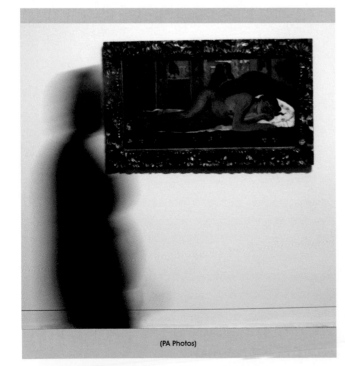

(PA Photos)

21st-Century Exhibitions

Gauguin: Maker of Myth was held at the Tate Modern in London between September 2010 and January 2011. It was the first time in more than half a century that the Tate had held an exhibition solely dedicated to the artist. The exhibition then moved to the National Gallery of Art in Washington between February and June that same year.

The exhibitions showed how Gauguin was an international traveler, influenced by the places he had lived in and visited, with works from his time in Brittany, his life in Paris and Tahiti, as well as the Marquesas Islands of French Polynesia. The paintings were chosen for the exhibition to show Gauguin's interest in the simpler things in life: the Breton peasants and the people of Tahiti – leading to Primitivism. The exhibition also explored the myths and legends in which Gauguin had a great interest, and was supported by the Gauguin Exhibition Supporters' Group.

Gauguin and Polynesia: An Elusive Paradise was held between September and December 2011 at the Ny Carlsberg Glyptotek in Copenhagen, Denmark, before the exhibition was moved to the Seattle Art Museum in the Simonyi Special Exhibition Galleries from February through April 2012. The exhibition was organized by Art Centre Basel and showed the artist's Polynesian influences, including 120 works comprising paintings and sculptures.

Van Gogh and Gauguin's Journey (Van Gogh e il viaggio di Gauguin), which was held at Palazzo Ducale in Genoa, Italy between November 2011 and April 2012, combined works from two centuries, from both sides of the Atlantic, with exhibits from Van Gogh, Gauguin, Edward Hopper, Caspar David Friedrich, Andrew Wyeth, and Richard Diebenkorn. The exhibit contained 80 great works, designed to show the physical and mental "journeys" undertaken by the artists in their groundbreaking achievements.

■ **LEFT:** A woman walks past *Nevermore O Tahiti*, 1897, at the Gauguin: Maker of Myth exhibition at the Tate Modern, London.

■ **OPPOSITE:** A woman looks at *Still Life with Three Puppies*, 1888, at the Gauguin: Maker of Myth exhibition.

(PA Photos)

(PA Photos)

■ **ABOVE:** A man looks at self-portraits of Gauguin at the Gauguin: Maker of Myth exhibition.

Further Reading

Paul Gauguin – The Complete Works
www.paul-gauguin.net

Technique and Meaning in the Paintings of Paul Gauguin by Vojtech Jirat-Wasiutynski: Cambridge University Press, 2000.

Van Gogh and Gauguin: The Search for Sacred Art by Debora Silverman: Farrar, Straus, & Giroux, 2000.

Gauguin by Himself edited by Belinda Thompson and Richard Kendall: Little, Brown, & Company, new edition, 2007.

Noa Noa: The Tahiti Journal of Paul Gauguin: Dover Publications, Inc., new edition, Nov. 1985.

The Yellow House: Van Gogh, Gauguin, and Nine Turbulent Weeks in Arles by Martin Gayford: Penguin, Mar. 2007.

Gauguin Tahiti: The Studio of the South Seas by George T. M. Shackleford and Claire Frèches-Thory: Thames & Hudson, Mar. 2004.

Paul Gauguin: Artist of Myth and Dream by Stephen F. Eisenman: Skira Editore, Aug. 2008.

Gauguin, the Origins of Symbolism by Richard Schiff, Richard R. Brettel, Guy Cogeval, Mary Ann Stevens, and Lola Jiminez Blanco: Philip Wilson Publishers Ltd., Nov. 2004.

Gauguin: Maker of Myth by Belinda Thompson and Tamar Garb: Tate Publishing, first edition, Sep. 2010.